LET'S GO PARTYING IN BRAZIL!

Geography 6Th Grade

Children's Explore The World Books

BABY PROFESSOR

EDUCATION KIDS

In this book, we're going to talk about the beautiful country of Brazil. So, let's get right to it!

WHERE IS BRAZIL?

About half of the South American continent's landmass is the country of Brazil. Most of the country is in the Southern Hemisphere and has a tropical climate. Its enormous rainforests are filled with thousands of different types of exotic animals and plants.

View of a Rainforest in Brazil

Tropical Beach in Brazil

Its eastern coastline is along the Atlantic Ocean and is over 7,400 kilometers in length with amazing beaches of golden sand. The sand isn't the only thing in Brazil that's golden. The country is rich with gold and other mineral deposits.

During the time of European colonial expansion, Portugal claimed Brazil and ruled there until 1822. The Portuguese people forever influenced the language, decorative art, culture, and architecture of the country.

THE BRAZILIAN PEOPLE AND THEIR CULTURE

There are three major ethnic groups that created the population of Brazil today.

- The Amerindians, who were the native peoples

- The Europeans, who were mainly from the country of Portugal

- The Africans, who were initially slaves

Brazilian woman of African descent

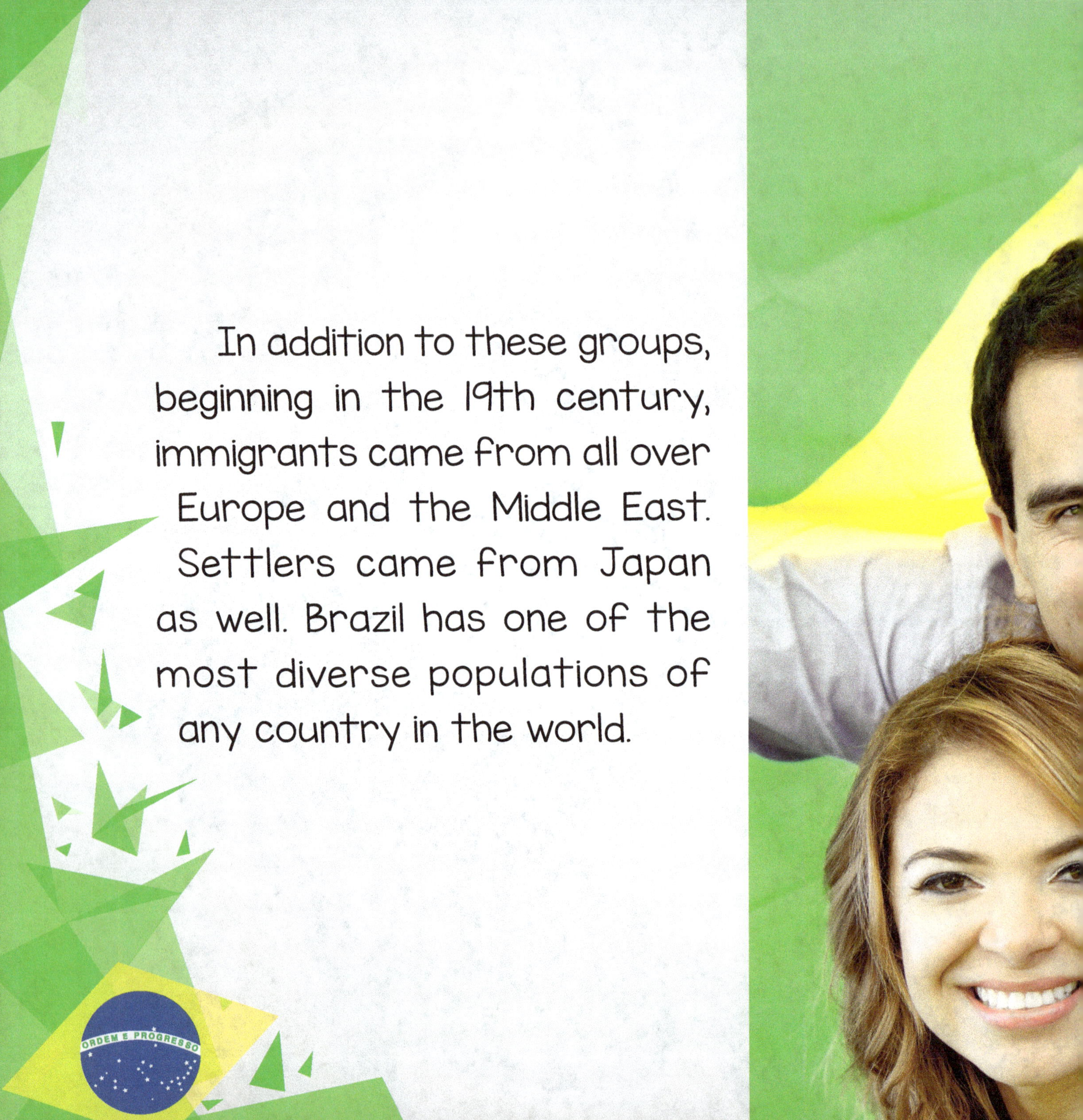

In addition to these groups, beginning in the 19th century, immigrants came from all over Europe and the Middle East. Settlers came from Japan as well. Brazil has one of the most diverse populations of any country in the world.

Brazilian soccer fans

There is one thing that everyone in Brazil shares and that is a love for the national sport of soccer. The Brazilians are crazy about soccer and their country has had the best soccer players in the world.

The most famous of their soccer players is Pelé. Brazilians have won the World Cup for soccer five times, which is more times than any other nation and they are the only country that has played in every tournament.

Now let's go exploring across the country of Brazil!

SUGAR LOAF,
RIO DE JANEIRO

One of the first things you see at Rio de Janeiro is the Sugar Loaf. It is a rock peak that rises to 394 meters in height. From the top of Sugar Loaf, you can see an amazing view of the city and its harbor.

SUGAR LOAF

The cable car to Sugar Loaf in Rio de Janeiro

You can take a thrilling ride on a cable car that's suspended between the peak of Sugar Loaf and a lower peak that's called Morro da Urca. From there you can take another cableway to the heart of the city. If you enjoy history, you can explore one of the earliest forts built in the city called Fort São João.

CRISTO REDENTOR, RIO DE JANEIRO

Diagonally situated from Sugar Loaf across the waterway is the amazing, colossal statue of Christ the Redeemer, which in Portuguese is Cristo Redentor. It is 709 meters in height and stands with its arms outstretched to welcome everyone to Rio de Janeiro.

Christ the Redeemer

Paul Landowski

This incredible monument was the work of Paul Landowski, a Polish-French sculptor and Heitor da Silva Costa, a Brazilian engineer. Created in 1931, it was designed in the Art Deco style and looks almost like Christ is emulating the cross.

Tijuca National Forest in Rio de Janeiro Brazil

The statue is located in Tijuca National Park. There is a railway that climbs the steep height where you can get out and walk around a platform at the base of the statue. You can also disembark from the railway at the midway point and explore the park, which is filled with tropical birds, exotic plants, and beautiful butterflies.

MANGUEIRA
Velho Juanda

CARNAVAL, RIO DE JANEIRO

If you would like to see a giant, colorful, street party, then you should come to Rio de Janeiro right before the season of Lent. Like Mardi Gras in New Orleans, Rio's Carnaval is filled with music and dancing.

Oscar Niemeyer, the most famous architect in Brazil designed the fantastic stadium there. It is called the Sambódromo. It's a very long group of grandstand boxes. There you can have a ringside seat for the Carnaval's parade route, which is 700 meters in length. Dancers compete against each other in the country's traditional samba dance in elaborate-looking, vibrant costumes.

Iguazu falls, Brazil

Iguaçu Falls

Where the country of Brazil meets the countries of Paraguay and Argentina, there is a spectacular series of waterfalls that are created by the Iguaçu River.

Some of these 247 waterfalls are 100 meters in height as they crash down to the gorge below. The most beautiful and widest panorama can be seen from the Brazilian side of the falls. There's also a bridge that goes all the way to one of the largest falls called Garganta do Diabo, which means Devil's Throat.

Devil's Throat

Capybara

The Iguaçu National Park is located near the falls where you can explore rainforests with a subtropical climate. More than one thousand species live in the park and you can see graceful ocelots, capybaras, which are the world's largest rodents, and fun-loving otters.

Copacabana Beach in
Rio de Janeiro, Brazil

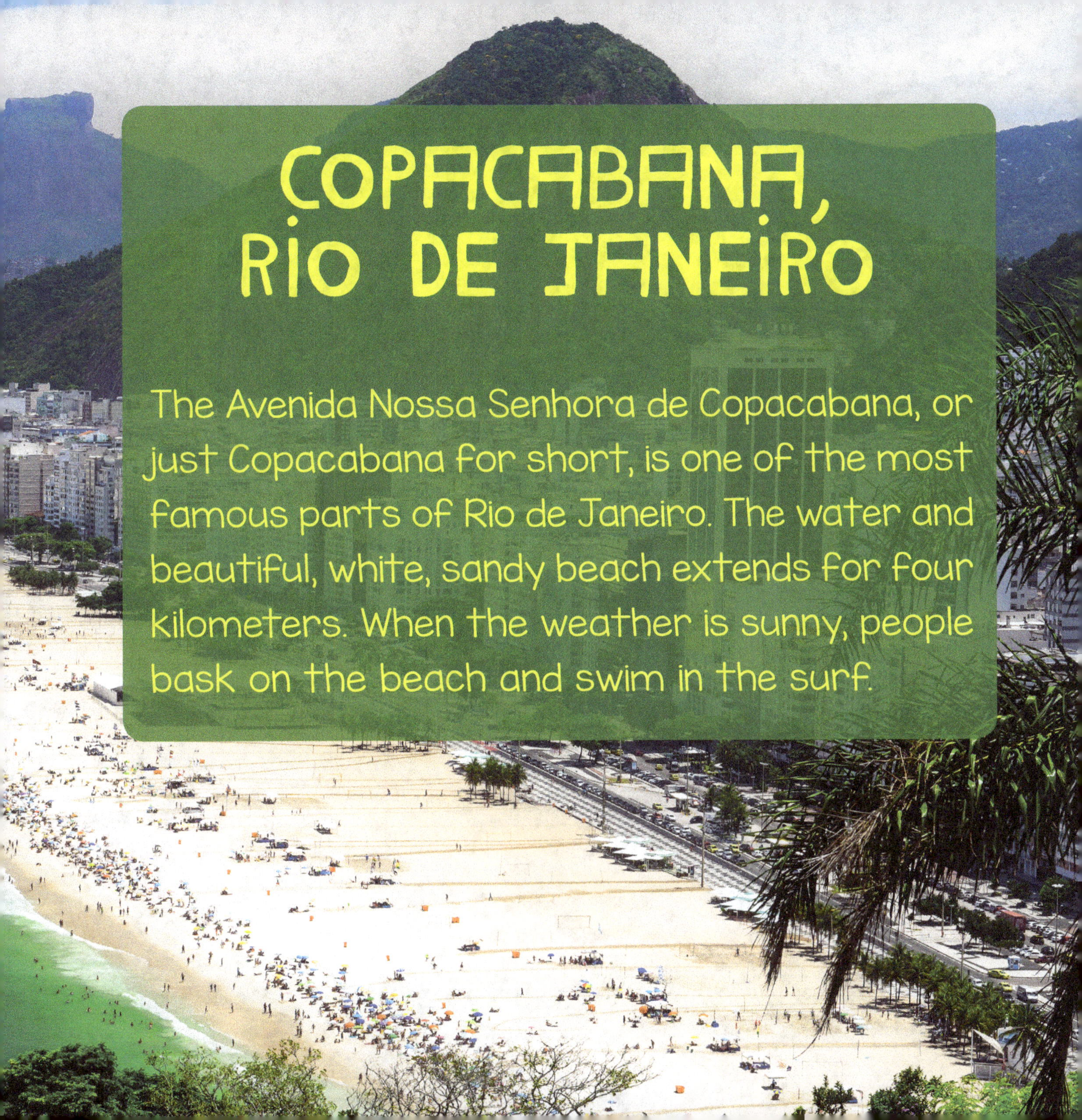

COPACABANA, RIO DE JANEIRO

The Avenida Nossa Senhora de Copacabana, or just Copacabana for short, is one of the most famous parts of Rio de Janeiro. The water and beautiful, white, sandy beach extends for four kilometers. When the weather is sunny, people bask on the beach and swim in the surf.

Iconic boardwalk at Copacabana Beach

You might like to build a sand castle with some Brazilian friends. Between the beach and the buildings is an amazing place to walk, which is called The Promenade. It's designed in a black and white undulating mosaic that almost seems to be dancing to the Brazilian beat. On the other side of The Promenade are lots of interesting shops and cafés to explore. There are also older buildings with interesting architecture that date back to when Rio was the country's capital.

AMAZON RAINFORESTS

Located northwest of Rio in the heart of Brazil is the city of Manaus. If you're really adventurous, this is where you'll want to go to visit the Amazon rainforest. The Rio Negro, which means "Black River," meets up with the Rio Solimõdes to become the "Encontro das Aguas," which translates to "the meeting of the waters."

Meeting of the Rio Amaturá (black water) and the Rio Solimoes (muddy water) at Amaturá in the Amazon, Brazil

The rivers flow parallel to each other until they mix to begin the mighty Amazon River. You can take a boat trip to the middle of the rainforests as you see amazing Amazon animals such as sluggish sloths, acrobatic monkeys, colorful parrots, and dangerous caimans. Also close to the city of Manaus is the enormous Janauari Ecological Park with its many different ecosystems. There is a large lake located there with giant water lilies that are unique to this region.

BRASILIA'S MODERNIST ARCHITECTURE

In 1960, the leaders of Brazil decided to move the capital from Rio de Janeiro to Brasília. It was a very ambitious plan, but it was achieved. The city was created in the wilderness within a time span of three years. Because it was planned from the very beginning, it has a different layout than most of the world's cities.

Brasilia

It has stunning, modern architecture, which is its biggest attraction. There you can see the circular building called Catedral Metropolitana Nossa Senhora Aparecida, which was designed by Oscar Niemeyer. The building, which is a church, has amazing concrete curved columns that support a roof made of glass.

Another of Niemeyer's incredible buildings is the Palácio dos Arcos, which is surrounded by lush gardens that were designed by Roberto Burle Max, a Brazilian landscape architect. Brasília has been declared a World Heritage city by UNESCO.

Pelourinho

SALVADOR'S PELOURINHO

In the city of Salvador, you can explore colorful colonial buildings that were built in the 17th and 18th centuries. This section of the city is called the Pelourinho and it is filled with churches as well as monasteries. The most elaborate of the churches is the church of São Francisco to honor Saint Francis. Gold is used throughout the church for detailed carvings. There are also beautiful tile panels of Portuguese design, which are known as azulejos.

PERNAMBUCO BEACHES

The section of the coastline at Pernambuco faces the Atlantic Ocean for a stretch of 187 kilometers. Many people believe that of its many beaches, Porto de Galinhas is the most beautiful. It has crystal-clear water, silvery sand, and towering palm trees.

Jangada

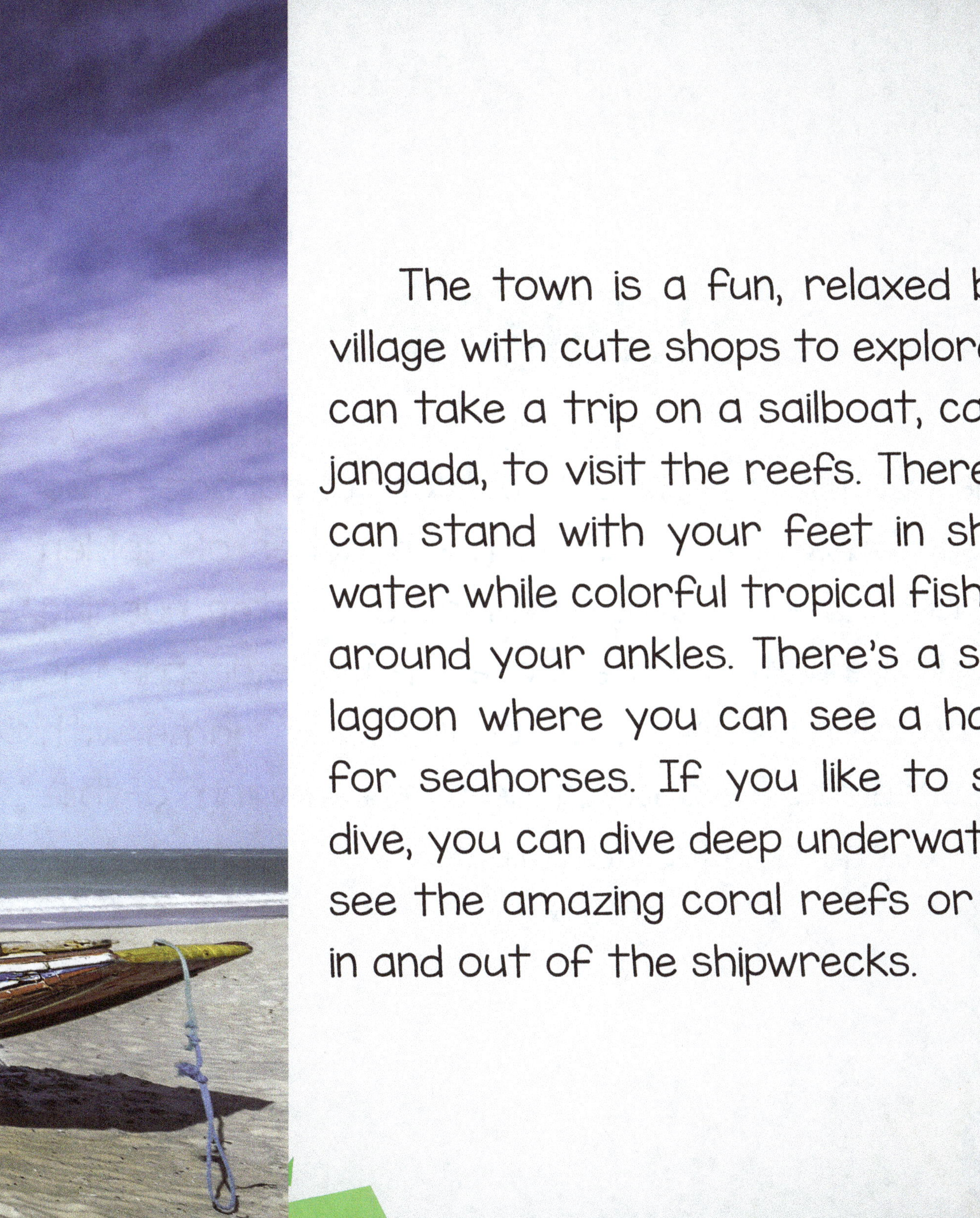

The town is a fun, relaxed beach village with cute shops to explore. You can take a trip on a sailboat, called a jangada, to visit the reefs. There, you can stand with your feet in shallow water while colorful tropical fish dart around your ankles. There's a special lagoon where you can see a habitat for seahorses. If you like to scuba dive, you can dive deep underwater to see the amazing coral reefs or swim in and out of the shipwrecks.

SUMMARY

The country of Brazil is a tropical paradise. You can bask in the sun on the beaches of golden sand, listen to the thunder of water rushing over the waterfalls, explore the jungle deep in the Amazon rainforest, watch a soccer game with screaming fans, or dance to the rhythm of the Carnaval in Rio de Janeiro.

ORDEM E PROGRESSO

Brazil

Awesome! Now that you know more about the country of Brazil you may want to travel to Australia and Oceania in the Baby Professor book *Australia and Oceania: The Smallest Continent, Unique Animal Life -Geography for Kids.*

Visit
BABY PROFESSOR
EDUCATION KIDS
www.BabyProfessorBooks.com
to download Free Baby Professor eBooks
and view our catalog of new and exciting
Children's Books